8 AMAZING POWERS OF PERSUASION!

8 AMAZING POWERS OF PERSUASION!

LEE BLACK

CONTENTS

INTRODUCTION **1**

1 Establishing Common Ground 5

2 Being Clear and Concise 11

3 Using Emotional Appeal 17

4 Using Logical Appeal 23

5 Asking for a Favor 34

6 Being Persistent 36

7 Being Willing to Compromise 38

8 Being Willing to Walk Away 42

CONCLUSION **49**

Introduction

This may actually be the most powerful book you will ever read! It will give you more than the just the power to change your life, it will give you the power to change the world! This is a truly extraordinary book because it unlocks an immense power, the power to persuade!

Your power to persuade others will have a profound affect on your life. You are about to see that when you are able to unlock the extreme power of persuasion, it can improve your life in many wonderful ways!

We all encounter everyday events where we need to be persuasive. For example, we may want to persuade a new employer to hire us, or our boss to give us a raise, or a customer to buy our product, or a co-worker to cover our shift, or a potential date to go out with us, or our spouse to go on vacation in a certain place, or our child to do their homework, or our friend to go to lunch with us, etc. In each of these situations and in so many other situations, we need the powers of persuasion to be successful and to get the most out of our life.

Persuasion is something we all do, but most of us have very little knowledge about how to do it effectively. Persuasion is something that is seldom taught in schools, we are not taught about it in high school or college, there is no class called "Persuasion 101." But persuasion is an extremely important part of virtually every aspect of our life and of our interactions with others.

Here you will learn the different kinds of persuasion methods along with examples of how to effectively use persuasion in your day to day life, and even how to use persuasion to change the world.

Some of the persuasion techniques discussed here are so powerful that caution is recommended before you ever use them! I must caution every reader to be considerate of others and not to take advantage of others once they gain the life changing powers of persuasion revealed here!

So to get started, let's first identify the 8 amazing powers of persuasion:

Establish common ground. Find something that you and the other person have in common, such as a shared interest or experience. This will help to build rapport and make the other person more likely to be persuaded by you.

Be clear and concise. State your case in a clear and concise way, without beating around the bush. This will help the other person to understand what you are asking for and why you are asking for it.

Use emotional appeals. Appeal to the other person's emotions, such as their sense of fear, hope, or pride. This can be a powerful way to persuade someone to do something, especially if the emotion is strong enough.

Use logical arguments. Support your case with logical arguments that make sense to the other person. This will help to persuade them that your request is reasonable and in their best interest.

Ask for a favor. People are more likely to be persuaded to do something if they feel like they are doing you a favor. So, instead of demanding that they do something, ask them for a favor.

Be persistent. Don't give up if the other person doesn't agree with you right away. Sometime people just need time to consider your request. Keep trying to persuade them, and eventually they may come around.

Be willing to compromise. If the other person is not willing to do everything you want, be willing to compromise. This may mean giving up something in return, but it can be a way to get the other person to agree to your request.

Be prepared to walk away. If the other person is not willing to cooperate, be prepared to walk away. This may seem like a drastic measure, but it can be effective in getting the other person to take you seriously.

Now let's look at each of these in more detail and see the secret to applying them to others. And we will see ways to combine these methods to further increase our power to persuade.

CHAPTER 1

Establishing Common Ground

Establishing common ground is a powerful way to build rapport and persuade others. Here are some specific examples of how you can use common ground to be persuasive:

If you are trying to sell a product to someone, you could start by talking about shared interests or experiences. For example, if you are selling a new type of running shoe, you could talk to the person about their favorite running trails and yours, or about your mutual running experiences.

If you are trying to convince someone to change their mind about something, you could start by acknowledging their point of view and then explaining how your perspective is similar. For example, if you are trying to convince someone that climate change is real, you could start by talking about how you both care about the environment and are open to reviewing evidence.

If you are trying to get someone to help you with a project, you could start by asking them about their skills and expertise. For example, if you are trying to get someone to help you with a marketing campaign, you could ask them about their experience with social media or email marketing.

Here is a story that illustrates how establishing common ground with someone can be used to persuade them.

Common Ground and Peace

In the land called the Divide, there was a long-standing rivalry between the two neighboring kingdoms of Larion and Meronia. The king of Larion, King Valdor, was a proud and ambitious man. He wanted to conquer Meronia and expand his power. He initiated a war with Meronia. The king of Meronia, King Anduin, was a wise and peaceful man. He wanted to avoid war at all costs, but also believed in completely destroying anyone who initiated war.

War raged between the kingdoms and dragged on for years. It all seemed hopeless but one person did not give up hope.

One day, a young woman named Anya came to King Valdor. She was a skilled diplomat and negotiator. She told King Valdor that she believed she could help the king to persuade King Anduin to sign a peace treaty because she was a well known singer in both kingdoms before the war. King Valdor was skeptical, but he agreed to let Anya try.

Anya traveled to Meronia and met with King Anduin. They talked for hours about their families, their dreams, and their hopes for the future. They also talked about the war. Anya acknowledged King Anduin's concerns about the war, but she also pointed out the cost of war. She told him that the war was destroying both kingdoms. She also told him that the people of both kingdoms were tired of war.

Anya made the following persuasive statements:

"We are all human beings, and we all want the same things: peace, prosperity, and happiness for our families and our children."

"The war is destroying both of our kingdoms. It is costing us lives, money, and resources. We cannot afford to continue this war."

"The people of both of our kingdoms are tired of war. They want peace."

"Peace is the only way to achieve our common goals. We can work together to rebuild our kingdoms and create a better future for our people."

King Anduin was impressed by Anya's wisdom and compassion. He agreed to meet with King Valdor to discuss peace. The two kings met and they talked for a long time. They talked about their common interests and their shared goals. They also talked about the horror of war that they both were experiencing. Then they agreed that the war was pointless and that it was time to make peace.

The two kings signed a peace treaty. The treaty ended the war and it established a lasting peace between the two kingdoms. The land was even renamed from the Divide to the United Kingdom. Anya was hailed as a hero for her role in bringing about peace. She had used her skills as a diplomat and a negotiator to establish common ground between the two kings. She had persuaded them to see that they had more in common than they had in differences. And she had helped them to realize that their desire for peace was their ultimate common ground.

Anya's story is a reminder that even in the midst of conflict, it is possible to find common ground. It is possible to build bridges between people who are different. And it is possible to achieve peace.

Seeking common ground not only is effective in peace talks, it also is an effective tool when used with other types of persuasion. "Common ground" opens the door to changing someone's mind, and it opens the lines of communication allowing an argument to be listened to.

Here are some more examples of how common ground can be used to persuade:

Situation: You are trying to persuade a friend to donate to a charity that helps homeless people.

Common ground: You both care about helping people in need.

Persuasive argument: "I know you care about helping people in need, just like I do. That's why I'm asking you to consider donating to this charity that helps homeless people. Every little bit helps, and together we can make a big difference."

In this example, the persuader is first establishing common ground with the person they are trying to persuade by pointing out that they both care about helping people in need. This is a powerful way to start a persuasive argument, because it shows that the persuader understands and respects the other person's values. Once the common ground has been established, the persuader then goes on to make their case for why the person should donate to the charity. They do this by highlighting the positive impact that the charity has on the lives of homeless people. By appealing to the other person's sense of empathy and compassion, the persuader is more likely to be successful in their persuasion attempt.

Here are some additional considerations when using common ground to persuade:

Be genuine. Don't try to force common ground that doesn't exist.

Be specific. Don't just say that you have something in common with the other person. Point out specific examples of your shared values or experiences.

Be respectful. Even if you disagree with the other person on some things, it's important to be respectful of their views.

Be patient. It takes time to build trust and rapport with someone. Don't expect to persuade them overnight.

Establishing common ground with someone will increase your power to persuade them. But it is just one of many tools that can be used to persuade someone. Now let's look at another key to persuasion, being clear and concise.

CHAPTER 2

Being Clear and Concise

Persuasion requires the attention and understanding from the one being persuaded, this is why being clear and concise in your communication contributes to the power to persuade. This may be simple, but it is also powerful.

For an example of effective and ineffective persuasion in every day life let's look at a business email sent to persuade employees to volunteer to help an employee rebuild their home after a fire.

Here is an example of a vague and unclear business email to workers requesting a reply of volunteers to help a co-worker rebuild their house that recently burned down, then it is followed by an email that is more clear and concise:

Subject: Volunteer for Coworker's House Fire

Hi everyone,

A fire in one's home can be a devastating experience for anyone. So I'm writing to ask if anyone would be willing to volunteer to help rebuild our coworker's house.

I came up with the idea that maybe the co-workers here could do something to help. So I was thinking that I would just send out an email to everyone about this. Maybe we could do something that will help.

As you know, their house recently burned down and they've lost so much. They're going to need a lot of help to get back on their feet.

We have never had a co-worker lose their house in a fire like this, and so I am asking for volunteers to help them. If anyone can help in any way, it would be appreciated. Maybe we will try to plan to do something sometime after work.

If you're interested in volunteering or helping some other way, then please let me know. Also let me know if their are any days or times you're available. We'll be coordinating all of the volunteer efforts through me.

Thanks,

Mr. Vague

This email is vague and unclear for a few reasons. First, it doesn't provide any specific details about the co-worker's house fire. What day did it happen? What caused it? How much damage was done? Without this information, it's difficult for workers to understand the scope of the problem and to understand how their help could be best utilized.

Second, the email doesn't ask for specific commitments from workers. It simply asks if they're "willing to volunteer" and then leaves it up to them to decide what days and times they're available. This makes it difficult for the sender to plan effectively and could lead to volunteers showing up at the wrong times or not showing up at all.

Finally, the email doesn't provide any sense of urgency. It simply says that the co-worker "needs a lot of help" but doesn't specify how much time they have to rebuild their house. This could lead to workers putting off volunteering until it's too late.

Here is an example of a more clear and concise email that is much more persuasive at getting volunteers and generating action:

Subject: Help Our Coworker Rebuild Their House!

Hi everyone,

I'm writing to ask for your help in rebuilding our coworker's house, which was struck by lightning and burned down last Saturday. As you know, Mr Burns and his family lost everything in the fire. They're going to need a lot of help to get back on their feet.

The fire happened on Saturday May 4th and caused extensive damage to their house in Yodaville. Everything but the garage was completely destroyed. Mr Burns and his family are currently staying with their friends, the Water family, but they really need their own place to call home. We're hoping to rebuild the house as quickly as possible, within 10 days starting this Saturday and working 9 AM to 5 PM each day.

So we are looking for volunteers to help with the following tasks starting this Saturday:

Demolishing the damaged house Saturday

Clearing the debris Sunday

Laying the foundation Monday

Framing the house Tuesday

Installing the roof Wednesday

Siding the house and painting next Thursday

Installing the flooring next Friday

Installing the cabinets next Saturday

Installing the appliances next Sunday

Final touch ups next Monday

If you're available to volunteer on any of the next 10 days starting this Saturday, then please let me know as soon as you can, but at least by tomorrow, this Friday. We'll be coordinating all of the volunteer efforts through me and starting the rebuild this Saturday.

We're also looking for donations of building materials, tools, and furniture. If you have anything you can donate, please also contact me by tomorrow, Friday.

Thank you for your help in rebuilding our coworker's house!

Sincerely,

Mr. Clear

This email is clear compared to the first example. It provides specific details about who the co-worker is, the damage done by house fire, how it happened, when it occurred and what actions need to be taken to help out. It asks for specific commitments from workers, it gives specific time frames, and it creates a sense of urgency. This is much more likely to persuade workers to volunteer their time and resources to help rebuild their coworker's house. And it is much more likely to stimulate positive change for the co-worker.

Next let's look at another way to persuade that is one of the most powerful, it is using an emotional appeal.

CHAPTER 3

Using Emotional Appeal

There is a very powerful persuasion tool that can overcome many objections, this persuasion tool is using an emotional appeal.

This persuasion method is so powerful that we need to be cautious about when and how we use it. This is because it often overcomes reason and common sense which can cause harm to others. Now let's look as some examples of this persuasion method.

Many people buy their car based mostly on the emotional persuasion of ads and sales people, instead of based on what is in their best interest. Emotional car commercials usually focus on the car being driven in a way that no one typically drives a car, or driven in remote areas that very few people ever drive to. The car ads have emotional visuals and music in an attempt to associate buying the new car as something that makes a person successful, happy, or powerful. But little is usually said about how practical the car is, how it will truly benefit the buyer, or what makes it a great value to the buyer.

Here is a story to illustrate how emotional persuasion may be used to sell someone something that only really benefits the seller.

Destructive Emotional Persuasion

John was in the market for a new car. He had been driving his old car for 10 years and it was starting to show its age. He went to a local car dealership to test drive a few different cars.

The salesman, Tom, was very friendly and helpful. He showed John around the lot and let him test drive a few different cars. John was particularly interested in a new luxury car that was on the lot.

Tom started to sell John on the car by appealing to his emotions. He talked about how the car would make John feel more confident and successful. He said that the car would turn heads wherever John went. He even told John that the car would help him attract women!

John was starting to feel tempted. He had always wanted a luxury car and Tom was making it sound like this car would change his life. But John knew that the car was very expensive. He didn't even know if he could afford it.

Tom sensed John's hesitation and he started to up the ante. He offered John a great deal on the car. He said that John could get the car for much less than the sticker price. He even offered to throw in a few extras, like a free car wash and a year of free oil changes.

John was sold. He couldn't resist the deal. He signed the paperwork and drove away in his new luxury car.

John was happy with his new car at first. He felt more confident and successful. He even got a few compliments from people about his car. But after a few months, John started to realize that he had made a mistake.

The car was very expensive to maintain. John had to pay for premium gas, expensive insurance, and frequent oil changes. He also found that the car was not as practical as he thought it would be. It was difficult to park in tight spaces and it was not very fuel-efficient.

John started to regret buying the car. He realized that he had been persuaded by Tom's emotional appeals. The car did not really benefit him in any way. It was only benefiting Tom, who made a big commission on the sale.

John's story reveals the power and the dangers of emotional persuasion. Emotional persuasion can persuade someone to ignore reason and common sense and take actions that will hurt them based on irrational emotions. This story also points out that when you are buying a big-ticket item, it is important to be rational and to make a decision based on your needs, not on your emotions.

Now let's look into the building blocks of emotional persuasion. What are the three major parts that create an effective emotional argument?

The three major ways to create an effective emotional argument are:

Identify the audience's emotions. What are they feeling right now? What are their hopes, fears, and desires? Once you know what the audience is feeling, you can start to tailor your argument to appeal to those emotions. For example, a politician might start their speech by talking about the fear that many people are feeling about the economy. They might say something like, "I know that many of you are worried about your jobs and your financial security. I want to assure you that I am working hard to create a better future for all of us."

Use language that evokes emotion. Choose words that will stir up the audience's emotions. Use vivid imagery, metaphors, and similes to paint a picture in their minds. For example, a charity might use words like "hope" and "love" to appeal to the audience's emotions. They might say something like, "Your donation can help to bring hope to a child who is living in poverty. Your financial love gives them the opportunity to go to school, to eat healthy food, and to have a safe place to live."

Tell a story. Stories are a powerful way to connect with people on an emotional level. They can help us to see the world through someone else's eyes and to feel their emotions. For example, a company might tell the story of a customer who was helped by their product. They might say something like, "Our product helped John to lose weight and to improve his health. He is now more confident and active than he has ever been."

When used effectively, emotional arguments can be very persuasive.

However, it is important to use this powerful persuasion tool responsibly. Emotional arguments should not be used to manipulate or deceive people. Emotional persuasion is something that has been used throughout man's history to change rational moral people into an irrational immoral people. Mobs of people may act out violently, and they may even kill others, who mean them no harm, in the irrational fire of emotional rage.

Two ways different ways emotional persuasion has been used in the past can be seen by looking at some of the speeches of Dr. Martin Luther King and Adolf Hitler.

Hitler used emotional persuasion to play on people's fears of enemies, both foreign and domestic. He warned of the dangers of Jews, communists, and other groups that he considered to be threats to Germany. Hitler used a emotional appeal to persuade people to hate and kill each other for his benefit.

But Dr. King used emotional persuasion for a different purpose. He used it to fight for equality and peace in his "I Have a Dream" speech. He spoke with such passion and emotion that he raised his voice to a shout at times. This passion helped to connect with his audience and it persuaded them to take action. Dr. King used emotional persuasion to fight for human rights and equality, and to create peace and love that would benefit others.

It is my personal opinion that emotional persuasion should be used in a responsible way that benefits people. Emotional persuasion can be a powerful force for good when used properly. It can connect people and help them to see the world in a new way.

Emotional persuasion may not be based on what is rational, its great power comes from emotions stirred up in the moment. Next let's look at the rational persuasion method, its has long term persuasive power, and how we can use it.

CHAPTER 4

Using Logical Appeal

Logical appeals are a very persuasive tool, and it can often benefit the one being persuaded. A logical appeals also has the benefit of being a more lasting persuasion method.

Let's look at the same story as above but change the persuasion method to a logical argument by a car salesperson trying to persuade someone to buy a new car.

Beneficial Persuasion with Logic

John was in the market for a new car. He had been driving his old car for 10 years and it was starting to show its age. He went to a local car dealership to test drive a few different cars.

The salesman, Tom, was very friendly and helpful. He showed John around the lot and let him test drive a few different cars. John was particularly interested in a new hybrid car that was on the lot.

Tom started to sell John on the car by appealing to his logic. He talked about how the car would save John money on gas. He said that the car would get up to 50 miles per gallon in the city and 60 miles per gallon on the highway. He also told John that the car qualifies for a rebate and was exempt from a state tax.

John was starting to see the benefits of buying this hybrid car. He knew that he currently spent a lot of money on gas every month. He also knew that the rebate and the state tax relief would save him a lot of money.

Tom continued to sell John on the car by talking about its other features. He said that the car was very safe. It had a five-star safety rating from the National Highway Traffic Safety Administration (NHTSA). He also said that the car was very reliable. It had a predicted reliability rating of four out of five stars from J.D. Power. And the overall cost of ownership was also quite low.

John was starting to feel confident that this hybrid car was the right choice for him. He knew that it would save him money on gas and that it was a safe and reliable car. John also liked the way the car looked.

Tom closed the deal by offering John a great deal on the car. He said that John could get the car for much less than the sticker price. He even offered to throw in a few extras, like a free car wash and a year of free oil changes.

John was sold. He couldn't resist the deal. He signed the paperwork and drove away in his new hybrid car.

John was happy with his new car. He saved money on gas every month. He also felt good about driving a car that was environmentally friendly and visually appealing. He knew that he had made a wise and logical decision by buying the hybrid car.

This story illustrates how a logical argument can be used to persuade someone to buy a new car. The car salesperson appealed to John's logic by talking about the car's fuel efficiency, safety, and reliability. He also offered John a great deal on the car, which made the decision even easier.

When used effectively, logical arguments can be very persuasive. It can help people to see the benefits of a desired decision, and it can ultimately help them to make a rational decision.

Logical argument just like emotional arguments can be used to benefit or harm others. So caution should also be used with this persuasion method.

The power of a logical persuasive argument method is that if done well it makes the other person feel foolish not to grant the request. And because it is not primarily based on stirred up emotions its influence persists over time.

There are two key aspects of making a logical persuasive argument. First you need to provide clear and convincing evidence to support your claims and request. And second, the evidence needs to be in a trustworthy form such as in the form of facts, statistics, expert opinions, or personal experiences.

Now let's stop for a moment to talk about the tremendous power that comes from combining persuasion techniques, and specifically of combining a logical appeal with an emotional appeal, and mixing them with establishing common ground.

The most power to persuade comes from using multiple persuasion techniques together. What comes next is literally the power to change the world. The following combined persuasion technique is so powerful that I hesitated to even write about it!

The **Holy Trinity of Persuasion** involves the persuasive techniques of **establishing common ground, using an emotional appeal, and using a logical appeal.**

We can see this being done all throughout history by leaders who changed the world, here are some examples of some of the most influential speeches in history and how they used the three persuasion techniques of **establishing common ground, using an emotional appeal, and using a logical appeal**:

1. Martin Luther King Jr.'s "I Have a Dream" speech (1963)
   This speech is considered one of the most important speeches in American history. It was delivered by Martin Luther King Jr. during the March on Washington for Jobs and Freedom, and it helped to galvanize the civil rights movement. One of the things that makes it so amazing is he held no political office and his race was looked down on by many Americans of that time, and yet he persuaded the entire country to change.
   King used all three persuasion techniques in his speech. He established common ground by talking about the shared values of equality and freedom. He made an emotional appeal by speaking about the dreams of African Americans for a better future. And he used logical appeals by citing the Declaration of Independence and the Constitution.
2. Winston Churchill's "We Shall Fight on the Beaches" speech (1940)
   This speech was delivered by Winston Churchill to the British

people after the Nazi invasion of France. It helped to rally the British people and boost their morale during a time of great crisis.

Churchill used all three persuasion techniques in his speech. He established common ground by talking about the shared experience of the British people. He made an emotional appeal by speaking about the importance of freedom and the need to fight for it. And he used logical appeals by outlining the challenges facing Britain and the need to unite in the face of adversity.

3. Abraham Lincoln's Gettysburg Address (1863)

This speech was delivered by Abraham Lincoln at the dedication of the Soldiers' National Cemetery in Gettysburg, Pennsylvania. It is considered one of the greatest speeches in American history.

Lincoln used all three persuasion techniques in his speech. He established common ground by talking about the shared sacrifice of the soldiers who had died at Gettysburg. He made an emotional appeal by speaking about the importance of freedom and equality. And he used logical appeals by arguing that the Civil War was a fight for the principles of democracy and self-government.

And last but certainly not least, let's look at Jesus and his power to persuade. Looking at the total history of man, Jesus is arguably the most persuasive person in human history, a person whose life we even base our time on!

Jesus used the same Holy Trinity of Persuasion in his speeches and it was a part of his life story too. Common ground is when he speaks to Jews about their common history and beliefs, it is also common ground when a divine being becomes a human and suffers the same things that humans do. The emotional appeal is his empathy and love for others. Jesus displayed a love so great that he endured much suffering and even gave his life to save mankind. And the logical appeal is that doing good and forgiving others improves life for everyone, and it opens the door to eternal life. The way Jesus used these persuasive techniques literally changed and shaped the world.

There is a caution that we all should take before using persuasion to benefit ourself, that caution is to consider if we are helping or hurting others. Caution is needed because combining these persuasive techniques has a great power to benefit or destroy people's lives, especially when applied to the masses.

In today's world we see how often persuasion is used to destroy lives for money. For an example of how persuasion may be used to benefit the persuader and hurt the persuaded, let's look at the many drug commercials on TV. These commercials are often using paid actors who smile, dance, and even sing about some harmful drug they want the public to buy. These drugs are often toxic substances that may temporarily fix one health or vanity issue while causing many more severe health issues to happen. And the end result of many of these toxic substances is a slow and painful drug dependent death.

The businesses aiming the destructive persuasive commercials at the naive public may know that no one should take their drugs. They may also know that simply eating healthy foods and exercising is much much better for the public then their toxic drug, but they sell the drugs anyway! They persuade the masses to use these harmful drugs just to make a profit, and they persuade law makers, government regulators, and politicians to allow them free access to pedal their deadly drugs.

A person can use the power to persuade on the masses to become quite wealthy or powerful. But they need to understand that the awesome power of the holy trinity of persuasion released on the public can heal or kill many. My hope is that the reader chooses to use all of the powerful persuasion techniques revealed here in a positive way. There are many ways to gain wealth and power for yourself using persuasion in a way that helps others, so why choose to do something that causes harm to others?

Now let's look at another way to persuade that is simple and easy to do, asking for a favor.

CHAPTER 5

Asking for a Favor

Sometimes the simplest things can be the most powerful. Sometimes the key to persuasion is just to ask for what you want, just to ask for a favor.

Here is an example of how asking for a favor can persuade someone to do something they otherwise would not:

You are trying to convince your friend to go to a party with you, but they are not really interested. You could try asking them as a favor. For example, you could say, "Hey, I know you're not really feeling up to going to the party, but I would really appreciate it if you came with me. It would mean a lot to me."

The reason why this might work is because people are more likely to do things for others when they feel like they are being asked as a favor. When you ask someone as a favor, you are essentially saying that you are relying on them and that you would be grateful for their help. This can make the person feel good about themselves and more likely to say yes. It is also important to be clear about what you are asking for and to be willing to reciprocate the favor in the future.

There are three key points to remember about asking for a favor.

Be direct and clear about what you are asking for. Don't beat around the bush or make the person guess what you want. Be specific and state your request clearly.

Explain why you are asking for the favor. What is the reason for your request? How will the person benefit from helping you? The more the person understands why you are asking for the favor, the more likely they are to say yes.

Be polite and respectful. Remember that you are asking someone to do something for you, so be polite and respectful in your request. Avoid making demands or putting the person on the spot.

Here are some specific examples of how you could use these techniques:

"I'm really sorry to ask, but I'm in a bind. I'm running late for work and I forgot my laptop at home. Would you mind dropping it off for me? I'll pay you back for your time."

"I know this is a lot to ask, but I'm really struggling with this project. I was wondering if you could take a look at it and give me some feedback. I would really appreciate it."

"I'm hosting a party this weekend and I need some help setting up. I was wondering if you would be willing to come over and help me out. I'll provide food and drinks, and I'll even give you a gift certificate to your favorite restaurant."

By following these tips, you can increase your chances of success when asking for a favor.

Now let's look at another thing that increases the power to persuade, persistence.

CHAPTER 6

Being Persistent

Persistence adds to the power to persuasion. Persistence means not giving up right away, it may also mean giving the person you are trying to persuade some time to consider your request before making the same request again.

Here are three examples of how someone can use persistence to persuade:

Keep trying even when you are met with resistance. If someone says no to you, don't give up right away. Try to understand why they said no and see if there is anything you can do to change their mind.

Be patient and don't get discouraged. Persuasion takes time and effort. Don't expect to change someone's mind overnight. Often if you just keep at it then you will eventually succeed.

Be willing to compromise. Sometimes, you may not be able to get everything you want the first time you ask. Be willing to come back with a compromise and to meet the other person halfway. This will show that you are willing to work with them and that you are serious about your request.

Here are some specific examples of how you could use these techniques:

You are trying to convince your parents to let you go to a party. They say no at first, but you keep trying to explain why you want to go and why it is safe. Eventually, they agree to let you go.

You are trying to get a raise at work. Your boss says no at first, but you keep talking to them about your accomplishments and why you deserve a raise. You do more research and later mention how long it would take to train your replacement and how much more they would have to be paid. Eventually, your boss agrees to give you a raise.

You are trying to convince your friend to go to the gym with you. They say no at first, but you keep asking them every week and telling them how great it makes you feel. So eventually they agree to go with you.

Persistence is the gift of a second chance that we can give ourself. In life it is a wonderful and rare thing to get a second chance at something. But being persistent gives you the power to give your requests a second chance. And this second chance increases your *power to persuade!*

Next let's see another way to increase our power to persuade, by being willing to compromise.

CHAPTER 7

Being Willing to Compromise

We are even more persuasive when we are flexible in our request. We may not get all that we request the way we would like, but if we are willing to compromise on some aspect of our request then we can increase the likelihood of being successful.

Here are three reasons that being willing to compromise can increase one's ability to persuade:

It shows that you are reasonable and open-minded. When you are willing to compromise, it shows that you are willing to listen to the other person's point of view and that you are not afraid to change your own mind. This makes you more persuasive because people are more likely to be persuaded by someone who they see as reasonable and open-minded.

For example, let's say you are trying to convince your boss to give you a raise. If you are unwilling to compromise on your salary demands, your boss is more likely to see you as unreasonable and not worth giving a raise to. However, if you are willing to compromise and say that you are willing to take a lower raise if your boss can give you other benefits, such as more vacation days or a flexible work schedule, then your boss is more likely to be persuaded.

It builds trust and goodwill. When you are willing to compromise, it shows that you are willing to put the other person's needs ahead of your own. This builds trust and goodwill, which makes the other person more likely to be persuaded by you in the future.

For example, let's say you are trying to convince your partner to go on a vacation with you. If you are unwilling to compromise on the location of the vacation, your partner is more likely to see you as selfish and not interested in their needs. However, if you are willing to compromise and say that you are willing to go to a location that your partner prefers, your partner is more likely to be persuaded.

It creates a win-win situation. When both parties are willing to compromise, it creates a win-win situation where everyone gets something that they want. This makes the other person more likely to be persuaded because they see that they are getting something out of the deal as well.

For example, let's say you are trying to negotiate a contract with a supplier. If you are unwilling to compromise on the price, the supplier is more likely to walk away from the negotiation. However, if you are willing to compromise and say that you are willing to pay a higher price if the supplier can give you a better delivery schedule, you are more likely to reach an agreement that benefits both parties.

Let’s look at a story about the power of compromise.

The Power of Compromise

A long time ago, there were two sisters, Alice and Barbara. They were very different from each other. Alice was outgoing and adventurous, while Barbara was shy and cautious.

One day, Alice and Barbara were arguing about what to do for the weekend. Alice wanted to go to the beach, but Barbara wanted to stay home and read a book. They argued for a long time, but neither of them would give in. They both felt powerless to come to any agreement.

Finally, Alice had an idea. She said, "Why don't we compromise? We can go to the beach for half the day, and then come home and read books for the rest of the day."

Barbara thought about it for a moment, and then she agreed. So they went to the beach for a few hours, and then they came home and read books.

Both Alice and Barbara were happy with the compromise. They had both gotten to do something they wanted to do, and they had also learned the power of compromise.

This story shows that compromise is a powerful tool that can be used to persuade others. When we are willing to compromise, we are showing that we are willing to listen to the other person's point of view and that we are willing to work together to find a solution that works for everyone.

Being willing to compromise can be used to persuade others in many situations. For example a parent might compromise with a child by letting the child stay up late one night if the child agrees to go to bed early the next night. Or on a larger scale, two countries might compromise in a peace negotiation by agreeing to give up some of their territory demands in order to get other lands and to reach a mutually beneficial agreement.

Compromise is not always easy, but it is often the best way to get what you want. When we are willing to compromise, we are showing that we are reasonable and that we are willing to work together. This can be a powerful tool for persuasion.

Now there is one final persuasion technique we will discuss, it is being willing to walk away.

CHAPTER 8

Being Willing to Walk Away

The last persuasion technique we will look at is one of the most powerful, it is the willingness to walk away.

How can being willing to walk away increase one's power to persuade? Let's look at two common but different scenarios to illustrate how to use this persuasion technique - buying a new car and asking for a raise. The following stories will illustrate each persuasion technique.

Willing to Buy Someplace Else

Sally had been saving up for a new car for months. She had done her research and knew exactly what she wanted: a red Toyota Corolla with a sun roof. She went to the dealership and found the perfect car, but the salesman quoted her a price that was $2,000 more than she was willing to pay.

Sally told the salesman that she was willing to walk away from the deal if he couldn't come down on the price. The salesman tried to pressure her into buying the car at his asking price, but Sally stood her ground. She confidently told him that she would be happy to come back and buy the car when he could get her the better price she wanted in the future.

The salesman eventually gave in and agreed to sell Sally the car for her desired price before she left that day. Sally was glad that she had been willing to walk away from the deal. But she also knew that if she had been willing to pay the higher price, the salesman would have never lowered it.

Just as the story illustrates, the willingness to walk away increases one's persuasive powers. Here are some of the reasons why it would increase your ability to persuade when you are buying a car from a dealer:

It shows that you are serious about buying a car, but that you are not willing to pay any price.

It puts the pressure on the dealership to sell you the car at a price that you are willing to pay.

It gives you more leverage in the negotiation.

It makes you more likely to get a good deal.

Now let's look at story about how this persuasion technique may be used by someone asking for a raise.

Willing to Leave My Job

Sarah has been working at a company for 5 years. She has been consistently meeting or exceeding her performance goals, and she has taken on additional responsibilities. She feels that she is underpaid and she decides to ask her supervisor for a raise.

Sarah schedules a meeting with her supervisor and she explains why she feels that she deserves a raise. She talks about her accomplishments, her willingness to take on more responsibility, and her commitment to the company. Her supervisor listens to her, but he says that he cannot give her a raise at this time. He says that the company is facing financial difficulties and that they are not able to give raises to everyone.

Sarah is disappointed, but she does not give up. She decides to do some research and she finds out that other people in her position are making more money than she is, including new hires. She also gets a job offer from another company that pays more than she is currently making.

Sarah schedules another meeting with her supervisor and she tells him about the other job offer. She says that she is willing to stay at the company, but she needs to be paid a fair wage. She also says that she is willing to walk away if she does not get the raise.

Her supervisor is taken aback by this. He knows that he cannot afford to lose Sarah, so he agrees to give her a raise. Sarah is happy with the outcome and she is glad that she stood up for herself.

In this story, Sarah was able to get a raise by being prepared, persistent, and willing to walk away. She did her research and she knew her worth. She was also willing to negotiate and she was not afraid to stand up for herself.

If you are thinking about asking for a raise or of making some other request like it, here are some tips to help give you the power to persuade:

Do your research and know your worth.

Be prepared to negotiate.

Be willing and ready to walk away.

Be respectful and polite, even if you get turned down.

If you are able to do these things, you will be more likely to succeed and to keep the other person's respect.

The willingness to walk away, like the other persuasion techniques, is most effective when used together with other persuasion techniques. For example just saying to your employer,

"Give me a raise now!" This is just not as effective as saying,

"I am making 10% less pay than the average inexperienced new hire is paid, but I have performed well for over 5 years now and have a great deal of expertise at my job. I am trying to support my family and my husband has expensive medical needs. I appreciate this company and my job, but I now have another job offer for 15% more pay which I will take if I can not get a raise. As a favor to me please see what can be done. I appreciate your time looking into this for me."

Which is more persuasive, the short demand for a raise, or the more detailed request? Obviously the request which uses multiple persuasive techniques is more effective. If the employer looks at it logically they can see it is more cost effective to give a raise then to replace the employee with a higher paid new hire that they must acquire and then train. From an emotional appeal the employee is struggling to survive financially, and needs more money to support their spouse. And on top of it all is the urgency created by the employee's new job offer and their willingness to walk away. All of these persuasion techniques used together gives Sarah even more power to persuade. It all adds up to more power to succeed.

This last persuasion technique when used with other techniques is extremely powerful. Of course with any persuasion technique there is always the possibility it will not work, but by effectively using them we are continually increasing our chance of success.

Conclusion

Now you have the eight persuasion secrets that truly give you the power to persuade. You can establish common ground, be clear and concise, give an emotional appeal, use a logical argument, ask for a favor, be persistent, be willing to compromise, and be willing to walk away.

Each individual persuasion method can change your life, and by using multiple methods you can be even more persuasive. In fact you can change the world!

I will conclude this book with a story where someone uses all of these persuasion techniques in one regular day of their life.

The Art of Persuasion

Art woke up early in the morning and started his day by establishing common ground with his wife regarding getting some things done before their vacation trip. They talked about their plans for the day and how they could help each other out. This helped to create a positive and cooperative atmosphere, which made it easier for Art to persuade his wife to do some of the things that he wanted done that day.

Later that day, Art went to work and had to give a presentation to his team. He made sure to be clear and concise in his presentation, and he used simple language so that everyone could understand. He also gave an emotional appeal, talking about how important the project was to him and how it would benefit the company. This helped him to connect with his audience and to be more persuasive in his request.

After his presentation, Art met with his boss to ask for a raise. He used a logical argument, pointing out his accomplishments and how he had exceeded expectations. He also asked for a favor, asking his boss to consider his request. His boss was initially hesitant, but Art had been persistently asking for a couple of months now and this day his boss was eventually persuaded him to give him a raise, especially since this day he indicated he was willing to walk away and showed his boss another job offer he has for more money.

Later that evening, Art went out to dinner with his friends to celebrate his new raise. He was willing to compromise on the restaurant, even though he really wanted to go to his favorite place. He also knew that his friends were on a tight budget, so he was willing to pay for the meal to go to the restaurant that he wanted. His compromise showed his friends that he was considerate and willing to put their needs ahead of his own.

Finally, Art ended his day by going for a walk. He thought about all of the things that he had accomplished that day, and he felt good about himself. He knew that he had used his persuasion skills effectively, and he was confident that he could continue to use them to achieve so many of his goals in life.

The next day one of his friends at work, named Pat, heard about Art's prior day, and he came up with a nickname for Art. The nickname became a popular term that started to be used everywhere where people spoke of persuasion. The nickname Pat gave to Art was "The Art of Persuasion."

In this story, Art used all of the persuasion techniques in different situations to achieve his goals. He was able to establish common ground, to be clear and concise, to give an emotional appeal, to use a logical argument, to ask for a favor, be persistent, to be willing to compromise, and to be willing to walk away. By using these techniques, he was able to glide through his day persuading others to see things his way, and ultimately getting what he wanted.

Now you have learned about the eight persuasion techniques and the art of persuasion. Your knowledge about this subtle skill will give you an immense power, the power to persuade! A power that will change your life and your world forever!

The End

&

Your Persuasive Beginning!

****

If you enjoyed this book then check out some of the many other books written by Lee Black such as the inspirational books in the "Black Magic Books Series" listed here:

Health Wealth and Happiness

Miraculous Stories of Health Wealth and Happiness

Conquer the Obstacles to Health Wealth and Happiness

How to Fit into Your LEE Black Jeans & Fill Them with Cash!

The Best Gifts to Give to Others & to Yourself!

And most recently see the books:

The Most Powerful Person in the World!

Ordinary Habits that Make You Extraordinary!

****

www.ingramcontent.com/pod-product-compliance
Ingram Content Group UK Ltd.
Pitfield, Milton Keynes, MK11 3LW, UK
UKHW021925190726
13853UKWH00002B/855

9 798868 923869